# Olympia

Publishers: George A. Christopoulos, John C. Bastias
Translation: Brian de Jongh
Managing Editor: Efi Karpodini
Special Photography: Spyros Tsavdaroglou and Makis Skiadaresis, Nikos Kontos
Colour separation: Pietro Carlotti

# Olympia

MANOLIS ANDRONICOS

Professor of Archaeology at the University of Thessalonike

EKDOTIKE ATHENON S.A.

Athens 1995

ISBN 960-213-046-6
Copyright © 1976
by
EKDOTIKE ATHENON S.A.
1, Vissarionos Street
Athens 106 72, Greece

PRINTED AND BOUND IN GREECE
by
EKDOTIKE HELLADOS S.A.
An affiliated company
8, Philadelphias Street, Athens

# OLYMPIA AND THE MUSEUM

## CULT AND GAMES: The ancient cult and myths of Olympia

Places, like men, have their destinies. On the remote slopes of Mount Parnassos, Apollo brought together the Hellenes under the Delphic Amphiktyony, and delivered oracles to both Greeks and "barbarians." There was, however, another remote corner of Greece, in the western Peloponnesos, which became the first home of athletics and whose name, as a result, spread throughout the world: Olympia.

The green landscape of Olympia, peaceful and serene, unfolds between two rivers, the Alpheios and the Kladeos (fig. 16). In ancient times, it was full of plane-trees and wild olives; in the dialect of the local inhabitants, the beautiful grove was known as the *Altis*. Whereas the god Apollo had found it necessary to lead men himself to the awe-inspiring rock of Delphi, the rich plain of Olympia was easily accessible and hospitable, as if asking to be chosen for habitation. It was only natural that men should decide to build their houses there at the beginning of the 2nd millennium B.C., or perhaps a little earlier. The apsidal dwellings discovered in the deeper layers of soil on the site of the sanctuary belong to the Middle Helladic period (1900-1600 B.C.). The first settlers knew nothing of Zeus and the Olympian gods. Tradition has it that the earliest cult was that of Kronos. This ancient god, father of Zeus, was worshipped on the imposing hill that dominates and bounds the northern side of the sanctuary. The hill was dedicated to him, as its name — Kronion — implies. At the foot of the hill stood other sanctuaries dedicated to female deities: Aphrodite Ourania, Eileithyia (and the dragon-shaped daemon Sosipolis), the Nymphs; finally there was the "Gaion," one of the earliest sanctuaries and oracles, belonging to the very first diviner, the goddess Gaia (Earth), and to her daughter Themis. We have no way of knowing when and how the cult of Pelops — the mysterious hero who gave his name to the Peloponnesos — reached Olympia, or why he became associated with the sacred Altis as the local "daemon," holy and venerable, worshipped next to Zeus. It is quite probable that his cult is older than that of Zeus, and that his *temenos* — the Pelopion — within the sanctuary, is the oldest known monument of the cult, dating back to the same period as the Hippodameion — Hippodameia's sanctuary — whose position is unknown to us. The ancient Greeks knew that this region, named Pisatis, from its capital, Pisa, was ruled by king Oinomaos, who had a daughter called Hippodameia. Before giving away his daughter in marriage, Oinomaos demanded that her suitor should defeat him in a chariot race. If, however, the suitor lost the race, Oinomaos would kill him. The king had killed thirteen such suitors when Pelops came to Pisa. He was the son of Tantalos, from distant Lydia, and his purpose was to take Hippodameia as his wife. During the crucial chariot race, he defeated the cruel king and married Hippodameia. This was how Pelops became associated with Olympia and was henceforth worshipped in the sacred Altis.

There exists another myth, however, which supplies us with clearly historical information. The myth says that when the time came for the Herakleidai to return to their fatherland, the Peloponnesos, they went through a series of mishaps and calamities. Finally, the Delphic god advised them to find a "three-eyed" guide and go through "the narrow pass." On their way they encountered the one-eyed Oxylos, a descendant of Aitolos, who had been king of Elis before going into exile to the land that later took his name: Aitolia. Oxylos was riding a horse, and therefore was "three-eyed." The Herakleidai asked him to guide them across to the Peloponnesos. Oxylos took them to Arkadia, while he turned west with the Aitolians and travelled to Elis, which was then inhabited by the Epeians. A battle ensued between the Aitolians and the Epeians and culminated in a heroic duel between the Aitolian Pyraichmes and the Epeian Degmenos; Pyraichmes emerged the victor. Thus Oxylos became once again king of Elis and the Aitolians lived peacefully side by side with the former inhabitants of the region.

The myth of Oxylos is a good illustration of what recent historical research refers to as the descent of the western Greek tribes into the Peloponnesos at the end of the Mycenaean era. It appears that the cult of Zeus dates from that time, and that he was worshipped as a warrior god, as shown by the early figurines representing him with a helmet. This warlike attribute is still manifest in the archaic cult statue of Zeus (*circa* 600 B.C.) which was housed in the Heraion, next to the seated Hera.

## The Olympic Games

It was only natural that the new cult of the "father of men and gods" should acquire a predominant place in the sacred grove and that the shrine should end by belonging mainly to him. But apart from the great altar, where the richest sacrifices were offered, there were several other altars in the Altis. Pausanias

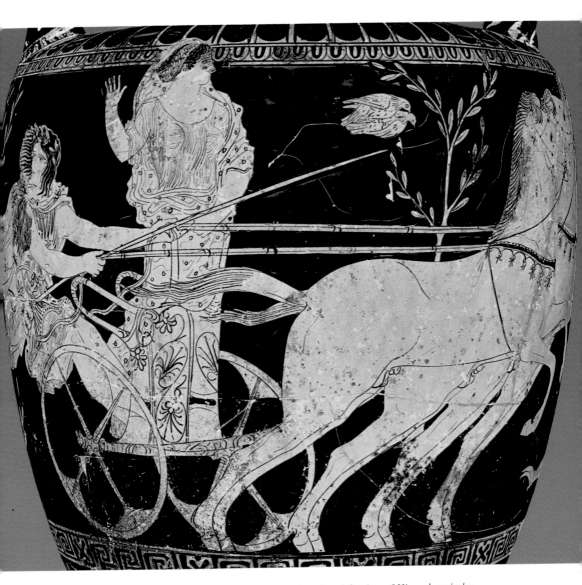

*1. Vase painting from the 5th century B.C. depicting the abduction of Hippodameia by Pelops in his chariot (Arezzo, Museo Archeologico).*

mentions 69, and we know he has not included all of them in his account. This means that Olympia was a sacred site where the ancient cults of the indigenous people continued to be practised next to the Olympian religion introduced by the settlers from western Greece. But this was not the factor that consecrated Olympia as the greatest Panhellenic sanctuary and determined its character and significance. Olympia owes its very special place among the other Greek sanctuaries to the games performed there every four years. The ancient Greeks ascribed the beginning of the Olympic Games to mythical times. This implies that the Olympic Games were believed by the Greeks to be of a most ancient

2. Wrestling scene on a red-figure amphora from the 6th century B.C. (Berlin, Staatliche Museum).

3. A discus thrower on a red-figure vase from the beginning of the 5th century B.C. The discus was an event demanding power, rhythm and accuracy, and was very popular in all the great games of ancient Greece (Munich, Antiken-Sammlungen).

4. Red-figure kylix from the beginning of the 5th century B.C. depicting athletes during the long jump (Boston, Museum of fine arts).

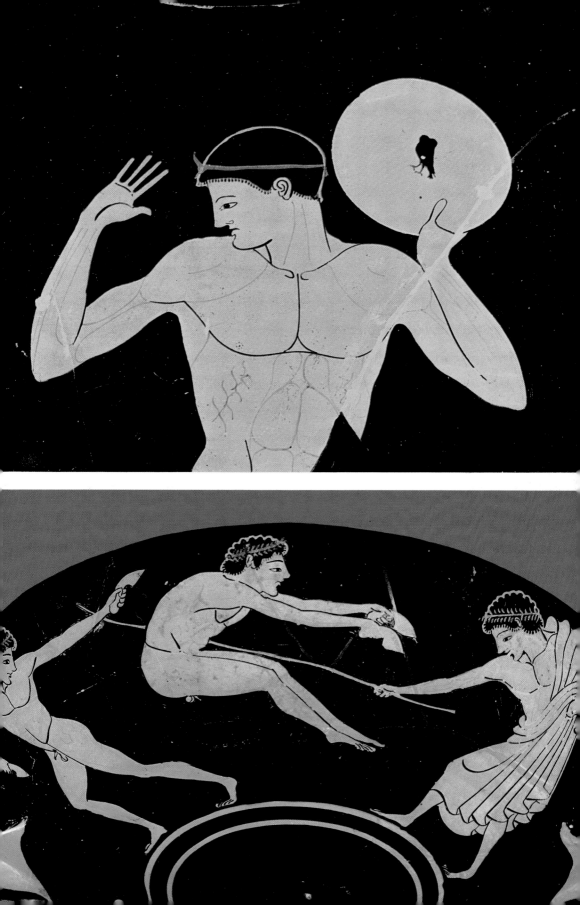

5. *Scene of a women's race on a black-figure* hydria *from the end of the 6th century B.C. The Heraia, which were women's races in honour of Hera, were held at Olympia every four years (Vatican Museum).*

6. *Athletes engaged in the pentathlon. Panathenaic amphora from the end of the 6th century B.C. The athletes depicted are a jumper, javelin thrower, discus thrower, and a second javelin thrower. (London, British Museum).*

7. *Scene of a men's* stadion *race on a Panathenaic amphora from the end of the 6th century B.C. (New York, Metropolitan Museum).*

5

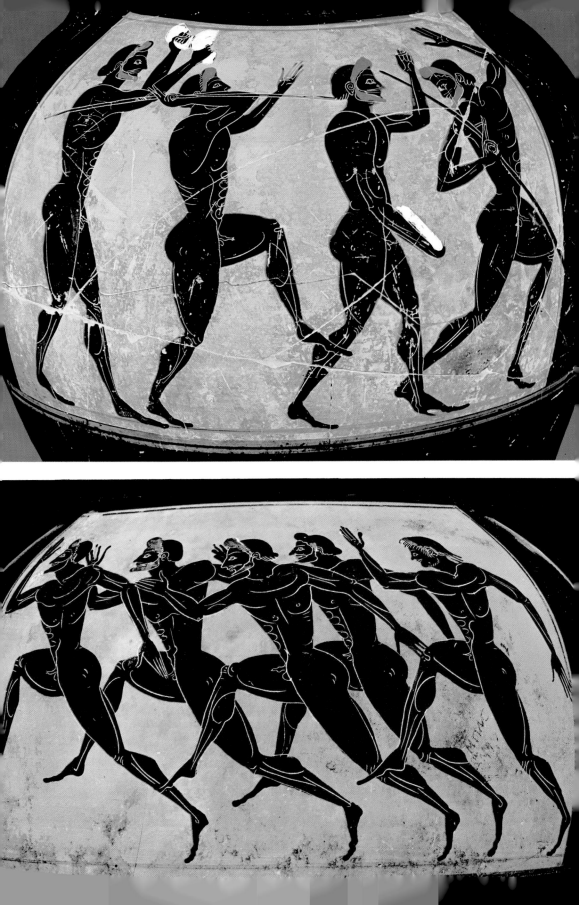

and sacred origin and that they formed an integral part of the ancestral cult.

Modern research is far from unanimous in interpreting the institution of the games. Some scholars believe that man's natural disposition to train himself and compete with others was the main motive that led the Greeks to introduce athletic games. But most scholars associate the introduction of the games with burial rites, because we know that in Homeric times games were held in honour of the dead.

However may one interpret the birth of the Olympic Games, their importance exceeds the limitations of both the time and the place where they were originally instituted. It is no exaggeration to say that those games gave birth to yet another Greek idea, a whole attitude to life — the attitude of a free man competing with his peers, naked, unfettered by any element foreign to his own body, conforming only to the rules of the game, with the sole aim of winning for himself an olive crown — in other words a purely moral victory – and the praise of his fellow-men.

## The significance of the Games in Greek history

The Olympic Games proved to be historical landmarks for the ancient Greek world. The year 776 B.C., which was the date of the first Olympiad, is also the first certain and accurate chronology in Greek history, because henceforth the names of victors in every Olympiad were officially recorded. The first victor was Koroibos of Elis, who won the one-stade race. But there is a second, far more important historical conclusion to be drawn from the Olympic Games: the Greeks, though divided into numerous tribal groups, though scattered over a vast area from Asia Minor to Italy and from Africa to Macedonia, though organized into hundreds of small states often at war with each other, had a deep awareness of their ethnic unity, which set them apart from the other inhabitants of the world. Only free Greeks were allowed to participate in the Olympic Games; that is why the highest officials and judges of the Games were named *Hellanodikai,* an ancient title that shows the supreme significance of the Olympic Games in the life of the Greeks. Their celebration demanded that all Greeks be present in peaceful assembly in the sacred grove. For this purpose the *spondophoroi,* noblemen of Elis followed by an official retinue acted as heralds travelling to all the Greek cities well ahead of the Games, in order to proclaim the *"ekecheiria"*, i.e. a truce, a suspension of hostilities that would last up to three months. Thus all the Greeks could proceed without fear to Olympia and attend the most splendid Panhellenic assembly, where they could not only admire youths excelling in athletic games, but also single out famous noblemen and illustrious sages, listen to poets and musicians, and above all mingle among themselves: the Dorians of Sicily with the Ionians of the East, the Greeks of Kyrene with their distant brothers from Macedonia. It is impossible for us to visualize that unique and

*8. Stater of Elis with a portrait of Zeus, the most important deity worshipped at Olympia. Middle of the 4th century B.C. Winged victory running to the left holding a crown in her hand, also on a coin from Elis. Silver tetradrachm struck by Philip II of Macedonia to commemorate his victory in the horse race in 356 B.C. It depicts the winning rider and the horse. (Athens, Numismatic Museum).*

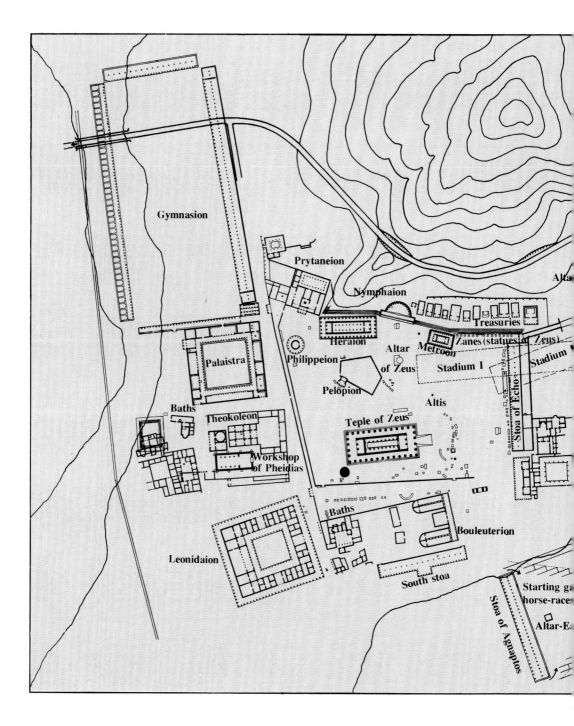

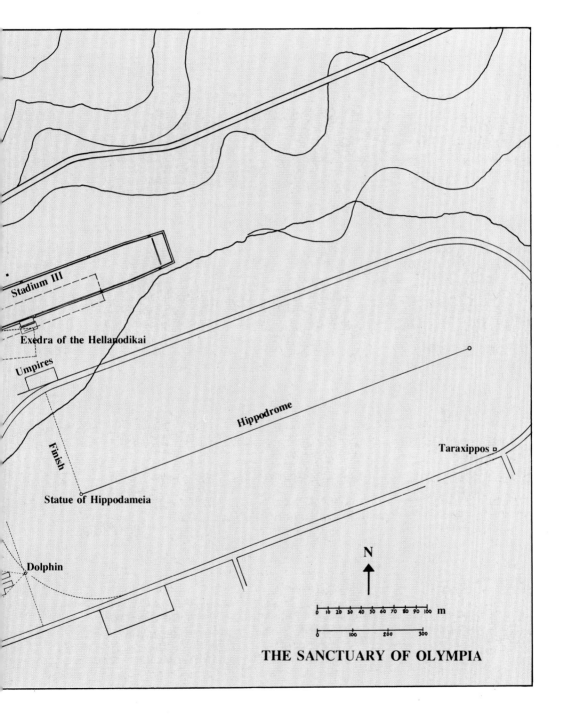

Stadium III

Exedra of the Hellanodikai

Umpires

Finish

Statue of Hippodameia

Hippodrome

Taraxippos

Dolphin

N

0 10 20 30 40 50 60 70 80 90 100 m

0 100 200 300

**THE SANCTUARY OF OLYMPIA**

*9. Reconstruction of the hippodrome at Olympia. On the left can be seen the hippaphesis*

soul-stirring 76th Olympiad (476 B.C.) when Greeks from all over the world watched Themistokles, the victor of Salamis, entering the Altis. Plutarch tells us that the whole day long, the crowds forgot about the athletes and the contests in order to acclaim the man who had led them to victory.

All this took place under the gaze and protection of the great Zeus, a warrior himself, who always stood by the Hellenes, whether in the struggles of war or in the peaceful contests of athleticism. In return, the Greeks, being a deeply religious people, offered him the arms which had brought them victory and the spoils of war which the god had helped them appropriate. The victors set up their own statues in the shrine of Zeus, not out of arrogance, but with the piety of those who can accept a god's gift in perfect humility. As the years went by, the votive offerings in the sacred grove grew more and more numerous, till they could be numbered by the thousands; they included precious and famed weapons which eventually made Olympia the most complete museum of the war history of Greece.

(starting gate).

## THE ALTIS: Architectural arrangement of the sanctuary

In Olympia, as in Delphi, many Greek cities raised "treasuries" in which to shelter their votive offerings. The treasuries here were not scattered within the *temenos,* as they were in the Delphic sanctuary, but were built in a row at the foot of Mount Kronion during the Archaic period (with a few exceptions). Apart from two of them, they were all offerings from Greek colonies overseas. However, it is noteworthy that until the early 5th century B.C., there was only one monumental edifice near the treasuries in the sacred grove; this was the very early temple of Hera (600 B.C.), in which Zeus was also worshipped (fig. 15). Two other buildings, the Prytaneion and the Bouleuterion – the former west of the Heraion and the latter at some distance to the south, beyond the sanctuary enclosure – did not singificantly alter the image of the shrine, which always consisted of the sacred grove, the altar of Zeus, the tomb of Pelops, the Hippodameion and of cource the vast *stadion* and the *hippodromos.*

17

Zeus, himself, the god of the sanctuary, did not possess a temple of his own. But in 472 B.C., when the state of Elis underwent a radical reorganization along the lines of the Athenian democracy, and when, a year later, the new capital, Elis, was founded as a result of a synoecism, it appears that the inhabitants decided to erect a temple to Zeus in the Altis. We know that the architect who built this temple was the Eleian Libon and that it was completed in 457 B.C., because that was the year when the Lakedaimonians dedicated to the temple a solid gold shield, which they set up on the akroterion, in commemoration of their victory over the Athenians at Tanagra. The dimensions of the temple were 27.68 m. × 64.12 m., which made it the largest in mainland Greece at the time (fig. 18). It was decorated with two admirable pediments and twelve metopes in relief, which are the most mature and powerful works produced by the severe style. A few years later, when Pheidias had completed his great works for the Athenian Acropolis, he came to Olympia and set to work on the gold and ivory statue of Zeus (12 m. high) seated majestically upon his throne.

It is from then onwards that the site began to be organized architecturally; numerous buildings appeared in rapid succession: porticoes, a *gymnasion* (fig. 20), a *palaistra* (fig. 21), a *katagogion* (guest-house), known by the name of its donor: "Leonidaion" (fig. 25); the elegant Ionic "tholos" built by Philip to shelter the statues of the royal house of Macedonia, also known as "Philippeion"; public baths, etc.; a multitude of votive offerings filled the empty intervals between the buildings, particularly in the area east of the temple. The fame of the sanctuary and of the Games persisted throughout the following centuries; the Romans added their own buildings and offerings to the already crowded site. The 293rd Olympiad was held in A.D. 393, i.e. 1169 years after the first. It was to be the last; the following year, emperor Theodosios issued the well-known decree prohibiting the practice of the ancient cult and the performance of the Games. A few years later, an early Christian basilica took the place of Pheidias' workshop (fig. 26).

## Excavations and research

In the 6th century A.D., a tremendous earthquake, such as often befalls the region, toppled to the ground all that had remained standing of the great temple. The two rivers, the Alpheios and the Kladeos, gradually covered up the ruins, protecting them under layers of silt till the day when the French archaeological mission of General Maison started digging up the site in April 1829. But systematic excavations began much later, on September 22, 1875, and have continued to this day, under the auspices of the German Archaeological Institute. These excavations were conducted with exemplary order and brilliant results, as was only to be expected if one recalls that among the first to participate in them were scholars like E. Curtius, and later on, eminent archaeologists such as Dörpfeld, Furtwängler, and more recently, E. Kunze. The first finds were numerous and important enough to warrant the creation of a museum. With funds supplied by Andreas Syngros and on plans designed by the German architects Adler and Dörpfeld, the Museum of Olympia was built in 1886; and it is this museum that still shelters part of the finds, all those that have not yet been transferred to the new museum which was recently opened and which allows a better display of the sculptures and the innumerable bronze

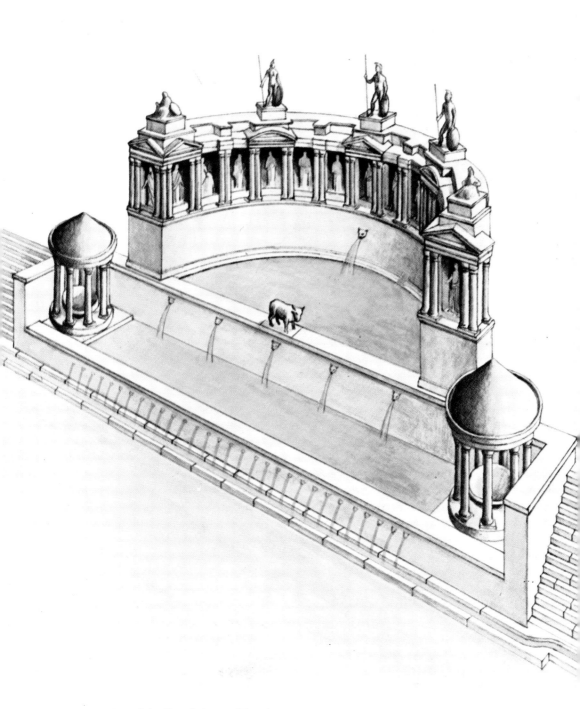

*10. Reconstruction of the Nymphaion at Olympia.*

votive offerings that represent one of the most valuable and rare collections in the whole world.

## THE MUSEUM SCULPTURES:
## The pediments of the temple of Zeus

We can fully appreciate the sculpture of the severe style (480-450 B.C.), when contemplating the Poseidon of Artemision, at the National Archaeological Museum in Athens, or the Charioteer at the Museum of Delphi. Works of this class are landmarks of the age in which they were produced, and they enable us to comprehend certain aspects of the severe style; but they do not provide an overall picture of the spiritual foundations and artistic conquests of this style. Fortune, however, has saved, for our delight, the most impressive group of sculptures embodying the claims and achievements of the severe style in a supreme and unparalleled creation: the pediments and metopes of the temple of Zeus at Olympia.

On the east pediment (fig. 38) the composition draws its inspiration from the myth of the chariot race between Pelops and Oinomaos. We see all the characters of the drama just before the beginning of the race; the two teams, Oinomaos and Sterope on the one side, Pelops and Hippodameia on the other, and next to them, the chariots and charioteers. Between the two teams, the imposing figure of Zeus forms the axis of the pediment. The "severe harmony" has never found a more appropriate aesthetic form: the vertical lines of the characters and the spears create a ponderous, hieratic atmosphere of tragedy in the centre of the composition, while on either side the chariots and the kneeling or reclining figures act as a frame, thus strikingly combining two elements that not only function differently, but antithetically; there is the same antithesis between the broad, clear surfaces of the central figures, which are conceived idealistically, as superhuman beings, and the realistic gestures and postures of the secondary figures (figs. 36-37).

The west pediment (fig. 39) depicts a Centauromachy during which the Centaurs, invited to the wedding of Peirithoos, a Lapith hero, get drunk and try to abduct the bride, Deidameia, and the other women present. This composition differs totally from the one on the east pediment. The incomparable figure of Apollo in the centre is the only one to maintain the vertical majesty of divine quietude; on his left and right, we see Theseus and Peirithoos, and then groups of Lapith men and women grappling with Centaurs, in a rhythmical and impetuous alternating movement, literally caused by opposite tensions, as it fluctuates incessantly from the centre to the two ends and back again, like the ebb and flow of the sea. The scenes depicted here are unequivocally violent, and the antithesis between the smooth virginal beauty of the girls and the bestial deformity of the Centaurs remains unbridgeable (figs. 40-43).

The contrast between the pediments is quite obvious to the spectator. On the east pediment, everything has come to a standstill, as if with suspended breath; forces are poised in expectation of the tragic conflict. On the west pediment, the conflicting forces have come to grips and are now locked in deadly combat. And yet both pediments are but a supreme expression, in plastic terms, of the tragic element. The power of tragedy is equally perturbing in both; it is only the expression that differs, in its selection of a different phase in the drama. On the east pediment, everything forebodes the coming catas-

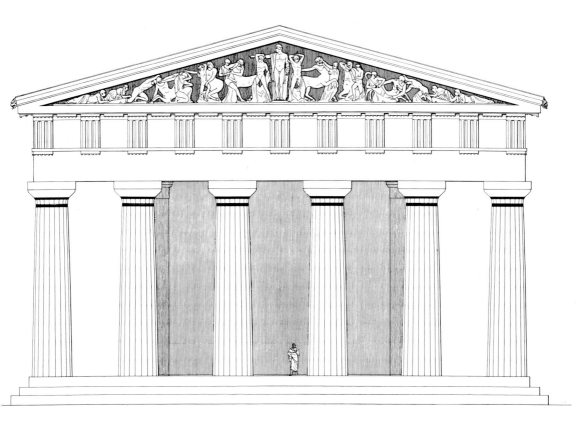

*11. Reconstruction of the west side of the temple of Zeus.*

trophe; the bride, who has broken away from her father's group to take up her position at her husband's side, already announces its outcome. On the west pediment, the imposing figures of the two heroes standing on either side of the great god of light, assure us that they will victoriously oppose the criminal violence of the Centaurs, with the help of the blessing expressed by the god's outstretched hand.

## The metopes of the temple of Zeus

The twelve metopes which were placed over the *pronaos* and the *opisthodomos* — divided into sets of six — represent the twelve labours of Herakles; for the first time in Greek art the *dodecathlon* becomes codified, so to speak. Some of the metopes have suffered severe damage, and three of them were removed to the Louvre by the first French excavators. However, thanks to intensive efforts, the archaeologists have succeeded in reconstituting several missing sections, so that we can now form a fairly accurate picture of the compositions and their plastic skill, which is indeed remarkable. The artist's imagination, wisdom and audacity, his flexibility, his wealth of expression have enabled him to obtain truly unique results, unsurpassed even, in several respects, by the metopes of the Parthenon itself. From the deeply exciting metope of the Knossian bull, with its conflict of forces, to the idyllic scene with

21

*12. Reconstruction of the east side of the temple of Zeus.*

the Stymphalian birds (fig. 46), from the unexpected version of the myth of the Nemean lion, lying dead at the feet of the exhausted Herakles, or the impressive and imaginative solution given to the story of the golden apples of the Hesperides (fig. 44), to the truly unique representation of the Augean stables (fig. 45), the conception, composition and execution in all these scenes convince us that we are in the presence of a genius, a creator of the highest order.

It goes without saying that a large number of craftsmen must have had a hand in producing this magnificent collection of sculptures; archaeologists have been able to pinpoint their various contributions in the figures of the metopes. However, as in the Parthenon later, towering above all these assistants and disciples, there existed a great artist who conceived, designed and supervised the execution of the three compositions. The highly original and noble conception of the whole work was the first, vital achievement; it took form in unusually bold and vigorous figures and their architecturally dynamic synthesis. We do not know who this great artist was; art historians, filled with admiration and awe at his achievement, admit their inability to determine even his artistic affinities; some believe that he belonged to the indigenous Peloponnesian tradition, while others suggest an island origin. However, as Sir John Beazley, the greatest historian of ancient art, only recently lost to us, might have said, the name of the artist is of little importance, since we are privileged to have before us his own work, which conveys the highest artistic messages, as well as the spiritual and religious exaltation of those distant times; one may safely assert that it shares the same degree of eminence as the poetry of Aischylos and Pindar.

## Archaic sculptures

These unique sculptures dominate the Museum of Olympia and make such a tremendous impact on the visitor that he finds himself unable to turn his eyes (or his mind, for that matter) to anything else. However, there exist in the museum a number of marvellous creations which mark the history of Greek sculpture in its most significant phases. For instance, the poros lion once serving as a spout, is one of the earliest – if not the earliest – works of Greek large sculpture, dating, as it does, from the period prior to the mid-7th century B.C.

The colossal head of Hera wearing a sacred headdress (*polos*) (fig. 29) takes first place in the history of Peloponnesian art, which was to produce in subsequent years a number of fine works. This head probably belonged to the very early cult statue of Hera which was set up in the Archaic Heraion, and which represented the goddess seated upon a throne, next to the standing Zeus. It is a creation of the early years of the 6th century B.C., practically contemporary with the Kouros of Sounion at the National Museum in Athens, with Kleobis and Biton at Delphi and with the sculptures of the temple of Korkyra. It shows us that from that early Archaic period, Greek sculpture succeeded not only in producing figures of a remarkable plastic plenitude and sensitivity, but also in representing the divine form with a combination of audacity and piety.

## Clay sculpture in the severe style

The centuries gone by have stripped the sanctuary of Olympia, like many others, of innumerable statues, that would have enabled us to follow step by step the transformation of form and content in successive representations of the god. However, we find some compensation for this great loss in the small bronze statuettes of various periods, which have fortunately survived in large numbers. By another stroke of good fortune, a few examples of clay sculpture have reached us; this kind of sculpture must have been fairly common in ancient Greece, but most of it has perished.

Only a few such works were found in Olympia, but they are comparable to the best marble and bronze sculptures, for their size distinguishes them from miniature art and places them in the class of large sculpture. There is ground to believe that the clay models which the great artists made before executing their works in bronze or marble (especially when the final execution had to be entrusted to apprentices or assistants), must have been somewhat similar to these clay figures. The colours that have survived on these sculptures also help us form a fairly accurate picture of the way ancient sculptures actually looked, before the passing of time turned them into cold, pure white objects that give an altogether false impression of ancient Greek art. It is enough to stand before the clay head of Athena (fig. 32) to sense the power concealed in this work; the face has been incomparably rendered; the flesh seems to pulsate with some inner tension; the sensitive, yet tightly drawn curves of the lips, and the flexible, watchful arches of the eye-lids and eye-brows framing the extraordinary inward-looking gaze — all this, crowned by the double row of curls in the archaic style, testifies in the most brilliant way how much Corinthian art had achieved in the later Archaic period, a few years before the battle of Salamis.

The finest of these clay statues in Olympia probably dates a few years later than the head of Athena (*circa* 470 B.C.). This admirable composition barely exceeds one metre in height; it probably stood on top of some pediment as an attractive akroterion. It represents the abduction of the beautiful Ganymedes by Zeus (fig. 34). The yellowish Corinthian clay of which it is made acquires incomparable warmth with its deep colouring. It is a daring and original work, which gives the great god a more familiar expression, less unworldly and awe-inspiring, without however detracting anything from his superhuman and divine character. Zeus is holding a traveller's walking-stick in his left hand; he is wearing a coloured *himation* which his rapid movement and violent action has displaced a little, revealing his chest and left leg. The "father of gods and men" is clasping tightly with his right hand the young body of Ganymedes. The boy is holding a rooster and seems to have abandoned himself to the god's will as Zeus pulls him impetuously to the left, heading for Mount Olympos, of course, where he will present Ganymedes with the gift of immortality. After the austere postures of Archaic sculpture, the statues fashioned in the severe style seem to be trying to exhaust all the possibilities afforded by the motion of the human body in its most vigorous and triumphant moments, thus obtaining an effect of unprecedented dynamism.

## The Nike of Paionios

Next to the unique examples of the severe style in the Museum of Olympia, the works representing the Classical age occupy only a limited space; they do not enable the visitor to form as complete a picture of Greek sculpture as one might expect from a site which was once overflowing with such works, as we are told by Pausanias and as we can ascertain for ourselves from the surviving pedestals, now deprived of the statues they once supported. Only two statues of the Classical period have escaped plundering; but they are so important and so representative that they compensate to a certain extent for the loss of all the others.

The first of these statues is a Nike (Victory) offered by the Messenians and Naupaktians in gratitude for their victory over the Lakedaimonians in 424 B.C.; it is known by the name of the artist who made it: the Nike of Paionios (fig. 47). It stood upon a tall triangular pedestal (about 9 m. high) in front of the east side of the temple of Zeus, and gave the spectator the impression that Victory, descending from her heavenly abode, was about to land on that very spot. This work is an exceptionally audacious achievement. It is the first time in the history of Greek sculpture that the flight of the winged goddess is rendered with such a keen feeling for the subject, without sacrificing either the plastic values or the structure of the work. The exquisite draping of the lower part of the *himation,* which counterbalances the two enormous wings, spread out wide open from the shoulder-blades, the marked inclination forward, impetuous, yet at the same time skilfully balanced, the suspended projection of the left limb,

*13. Reconstruction of the Nike of Paionios.*

the slight bending of the head – all this is welded together into a composition that is full of vitality and majesty, not devoid, however, of grace and feminine refinement.

## The Hermes of Praxiteles

A little further away stands the second Classical statue, perhaps the most renowned work of ancient Greek sculpture: the Hermes of Praxiteles (fig. 48). His fame is so great that he hardly needs our introduction. Though a few archaeologists doubt his authenticity insisting that it is but an admirable Roman copy of the Praxitelian masterpiece, most scholars believe it to be the original, with a few interferences on the back part of the body which are due to a number of causes. The ravages of time have fortunately spared not only the slender body of the god, but also his face, with its pensive, humid gaze, the opulent, finely chiselled hair, the gentle curves of the brow and cheeks. However, if one is coming from the hall where the austere pedimental sculptures are exhibited and pauses before this lithe, rather soft body, produced in the late 4th century B.C., that is to say in an age of greater experience, yet weary from the long progress through the years, one inevitably finds it difficult to pass judgement and to adapt oneself to this new artistic climate. But whoever has resolved to travel through the immense scenery of the history of art must know that he is bound to encounter all kinds of flower and fruit, all equally important and valuable, and that he must not be taken aback by the unexpected shifts and changes he will find. This is precisely what makes for the inexhaustible wealth of art.

## THE FINDS FROM THE WORKSHOP OF PHEIDIAS

Before we move on to the unique collection of bronzes in the Museum of Olympia, we must pause for a while before some small and rather strange ceramic objects, some ivory and glass fragments and finally some very fine tools which together with an apparently insignificant small vase constitute the most exciting find of recent years. As already mentioned, the famous gold and ivory statue of Zeus, a work of Pheidias, stood within the temple of that god. From traditional sources we have located the place where the great sculptor had built his workshop; it is the spot where a Christian basilica was erected in later years. Although many scholars had contested the reliability of this information, research finally confirmed its exactitude. The excavations of the German Archaeological Institute on the workshop's site brought to light tangible proof of the work of Pheidias: a number of clay moulds that were used to give shape to the draperies of Zeus' gold *himation*. Various tools for the carving of gold and ivory and several ivory fragments complete this unique find. Though the major work is lost to us — it was removed, in the late 4th century A.D., to Constantinople where it was later destroyed by fire — we still have these moulds; they give us an idea of the manner in which the great statue was executed, and will perhaps enable us to reconstruct part of it.

But apart from this, the excavation of the workshop held in store an unbelievable surprise; it has yielded the most moving finds that one could possibly

*14. Reconstruction of the chryselephantine cult statue of Zeus at Olympia, by Pheidias.*

imagine. Among the numerous sherds that were found on the site, there were a few that belonged to a very small, plain wine-jug (*oinochoe*). After these had been cleaned and mended, archaeologists were able to read an inscription engraved on the outer surface at the bottom of the vessel; it was written in beautiful lettering and consisted of only two words: ΦΕΙΔΙΟ ΕΙΜΙ (=I belong to Pheidias).

And so we held in our hands, after 2400 years, the very jug that the almost legendary artist kept in his workshop to quench his thirst whenever the heat of Olympia and the arduousness of his work dried his lips. With our fingers we touched his own touch, as the poet Seferis would have said.

## THE MUSEUM BRONZES:
## The bronze statuettes

The old guides to Olympia mention the existence of fourteen thousand bronze objects. If we add to these all the items transferred to the National Archaeological Museum in Athens and those discovered in recent years, we will have some idea of the wealth of these bronzes and of the importance of the Museum of Olympia, in the research and study of the art of bronze work in ancient Greece. Indeed, it is particularly significant that the bronze finds of Olympia represent all the successive periods of Greek civilization, from the Geometric age to the end of antiquity, as well as all the various Greek workshops: Ionian, Peloponnesian, Attic and South Italian. These bronze objects also include all the different products of bronzework: figurines, vessels, jewellery, weapons, architectural ornament, etc. Finally, there exist- in this splendidly rich collection extremely rare examples of the technique of hammered bronze, used for relatively large sculptures. This technique was employed by Greek bronzeworkers until approximately the mid-6th century B.C., in other words until the period when two artists from Samos, Rhoikos and Theodoros, invented hollow bronze-casting. The hammered bronze sculpture discovered at Olympia represents a single-winged figure, slightly smaller than life-size (fig. 49). With its rounded face and wide-open eyes — made of inlaid wood — this strange figure is a good example of bronzework in the first decades of the 6th century B.C.

We have already said that the statuettes compensate to some extent for the loss of the major sculptural works dedicated to Zeus, because their size does not in any way detract from their quality, which in some cases is remarkably high. For instance, the small figure of a bearded warrior, with a large sword on his left side, is an exquisite product of the Lakonian workshop in the mid-6th century B.C. (fig. 50). This figure, together with another surviving figure of a bald old man and several others, adorned the rim of a huge bronze vessel, most probably a krater, presented as a votive offering to the sacred grove. We know that the Lakonian bronze workshop was famous for its high skill in the Archaic period, and that it was particularly renowned for its kraters.

The Argive workshop was equally famous during that period; it maintained its reputation and high quality well into the Classical age, when it won an eminent position thanks to its outstanding artist Polykleitos and his descendants. One has only to look at the tiny statuette of a runner, arms outstretched and left knee slightly bent forward in preparation for the race, to understand how the Argive craftsmen succeeded in rendering, economically and effectively, both the athletic body and the elusive moment of self-propulsion (fig.

51). The inscription on the runner's right thigh "I belong to Zeus" suggests that the statuette was presented as an offering to the patron of the Olympic Games by some athlete in the years 480 - 470 B.C.

The small figure of a horse (fig. 52) — once part of a composition representing a four-horse chariot — also seems to have originated from the Argive workshop. Like the runner, it was dedicated, a few years later (470-460 B.C.), to the sanctuary of Zeus. The austere posture of the horse's body, the simple yet skilful workmanship, the precision and sureness of touch in rendering the details of the head, place this work in the very first rank of creations in the severe style and enable us to visualize all those impressive bronze four-horse chariots dedicated by the rich archons of Sicily to the Panhellenic sanctuaries, such as the one from which the Delphi Charioteer originates.

## Bronze sheets

Pausanias, the traveller of the 2nd century A.D. whose writings have proved so invaluable to us, describes in great detail, among the many things he saw at Olympia, a sarcophagus made of cedar-wood. It was placed in the temple of Hera, a votive offering from the Kypselidai, the famous tyrants of Corinth in the early 6th century B.C., and it bore some representations in ivory and gold, and others engraved on the wood itself. Pausanias then goes on to describe the numerous Greek myths that were illustrated on it. The sarcophagus itself has not survived; but the sanctuary of Olympia yielded hundreds of bronze sheets with relief representations of great variety, which are not only admirable examples of Greek bronzework, but also offer a very early and lavish illustration of Greek myths. Many of these sheets are probably remnants from wooden sarcophagi like the one described by Pausanias or from wooden tablets, while some of the others were used as decorations for tripod legs or shield handles. On a bronze sheet belonging to a tripod of the 8th century B.C., we can see the earliest representation of the myth of the Delphic tripod, which Herakles attempted to take away in order to found an oracle of his own. However, the most interesting bronze sheets date from the 7th and 6th century B.C.; in many of these, archaeologists believe they can discern the technique of Ionian art as practised in the Cyclades, or of the eastern workshops of Samos, Chios, etc. This does not necessarily imply that they came to Olympia from those particular regions, because we are well aware that in the early Archaic period, several Ionian craftsmen worked in the Peloponnesos; it is not improbable that some of them even founded workshops in Olympia itself, where their work must have been in great demand.

Be that as it may, the works themselves are what matters most, the sensitiveness of the reliefs, the enchanting way they tell their stories. In one of the earliest bronze sheets (*circa* 630 B.C.), we see two Centaurs holding fir branches, and between them an armed warrior, whose feet seem to disappear into the ground from the middle of the calves down (fig. 53). An ancient spectator would immediately recognize here the myth of Kaineus, the hero who had been made immortal and whom the Centaurs wished to exterminate by nailing him into the ground with the help of fir-trunks. The representation of a warrior departing for the battlefield which we see on another bronze plate must also be mythological; before mounting his chariot, where the charioteer is already holding the reins, the warrior turns his head to throw a last glance at his wife, who is carrying a child in her arms and bidding him farewell (fig. 54). It is not easy to say which of the innumerable heroes who departed again and again on military expeditions the artist had in mind in those early decades of the 6th century B.C. What is certain, however, is that he succeeded in rendering the emotional atmosphere of such a moment simply and effectively, with restrained yet highly expressive gestures and attitudes. The two scenes that are depicted, one above the other, on a third bronze sheet, of a later date than the two previous ones (*circa* 570 B.C.), are even more concentrated and dramatic. In the scene at the bottom, Theseus is shown abducting Antiope, while in the upper scene, Orestes is seen killing his mother, Klytaimnestra (fig. 55). The characters' gestures have now grown intense and passionate as befits the themes represented; the compositions have a thematic and artistic self-sufficiency such as we can only encounter later in the relief metopes of Greek temples.

## Bronze weapons

All the objects we have just mentioned were votive offerings to the god, or *agalmata* as the Greeks of the Archaic period used to call them, for they were intended to make the god rejoice. But nothing could cause a warrior god, such as Zeus of Olympia, to rejoice more than a gift of splendid weapons. Therefore mortal warriors who also loved weapons, and wished them to be not only strong and enduring for the battle, but also beautiful to look at, so that they could take pride and pleasure in wearing them, offered their arms to the god unsparingly, in their wish to thank him for the victory he had granted them or the victory they hoped to win. Thus the *chalkotheke* (bronze-store) of Olympia possesses the richest and finest collection of ancient Greek weapons of every kind. It contains real masterpieces which astound the modern, practically-minded visitor with their unbelievably ingenious and inspired ornamentation.

## Breastplates

One of the most outstanding pieces, from every point of view, is the bronze breastplate which came to light in the last century in the bed of the river Alpheios, became part of a private collection in Zakynthos and finally disappeared. Some archaeologists made drawings of it in 1883 in order to study the admirable representations engraved on it. Quite unexpectedly, it made its appearance again in 1969, at an auction of antiquities in Switzerland. Thanks to private contributions, it was purchased and brought back to the place where it had first been dedicated, in the middle of the 7th century B.C., by some rich sovereign, perhaps one of the famous "tyrants" that ruled a number of Greek cities throughout the 7th century B.C. Six figures are drawn on the lower part of the breastplate; on the right, Apollo with his lyre, and behind him two girls, possibly the Hyperborean maidens; on the left, Zeus, with two young men standing behind him. In the upper part of the breastplate, there are lions, bulls and sphinxes (fig. 59). The clear, sensitive design, the rich attire of the figures, the love of ornamental detail betray the Ionian origin of the artist.

There is another magnificent breastplate, which archaeologists ascribe to a Cretan workshop. It is of a slightly earlier date than the first one and was discovered at Olympia not very long ago; it represents Helen among her two brothers, the Dioskouroi.

Such superior pieces were naturally not the usual equipment of warriors, even the wealthier ones. However, the simplest and most inexpensive of breastplates testify to the exceptional skill and artistic sensitivity of Greek bronze workers. This is evidenced by a breastplate of the first half of the 6th century B.C., which is relatively unadorned, but beautifully made and shaped (fig. 58).

## Greaves and helmets

Greaves were a necessary complement to an ancient warrior's armour. This simple protective covering for the legs was given such striking artistic form that it became an incomparable work of art, instructing us about the ways in which an artist's feeling for form can give life to the lines and volumes of an object (fig. 57). The same creative force is present in the innumerable helmets found on the site of Olympia. If one compares them to the hopelessly uniform and expressionless helmets of our modern soldiers, one cannot help being amazed to see that hardly any two of them are alike. Each helmet is a unique creation, and its decoration, always strictly conforming to the dictates of its form and functional requirements, converts it into a delightful work of art (figs. 60-64).

But beyond their artistic and technical interest, some helmets and other weapons have a unique historical significance, for they evoke in the most tangible way dramatic moments in ancient Greek history. For instance, oxidation has destroyed the upper part of a helmet of the common Corinthian type; it is simple and unadorned, so that one might easily walk past it without giving it much attention, unless one happens to read the inscription engraved on the edge of the cheek-piece "Miltiades presented this to Zeus" (fig. 60). A simple name, all by itself, without a patronym or place of origin, as was the custom among the ancient Greeks. But who needed this additional information in order to recognize the helmet of Miltiades, the glorious Athenian general, the victor of Marathon, known to all the Greeks? This must have been the helmet he wore when he fought his great battle. He then offered it, humbly and reverently, to the god at Olympia. Next to it, we see another helmet, a foreign-looking one this time, standing out among the numerous Greek helmets of various types. Here too, there is an inscription on the cheek-piece, which proudly answers our question: "To Zeus from the Athenians, who took it from the Medes" (fig. 61). The helmet of the victorious general and the spoil of a vanquished enemy were thus preserved by the soil of Olympia, and now provide us with this unexpected contact with the first legendary victory of the Greeks at Marathon.

## Shield devices

Ornamentation on helmets and greaves was necessarily limited and of secondary importance; but with shields it was a different matter; artists had plenty of scope to display all their skill and imagination. The circular surface of the shield could be decorated with a central ornamental design known as *episema* (device or insignia). A large number of such devices have been found at Olympia, giving us an idea of the wealth of decorative themes devised by the artists of that time. One of the most adaptable, and therefore popular, motifs was Gorgo and the Gorgoneia; for the ancient Greeks, these creatures possessed a hideous power, which was supposed to enhance the defensive properties of the shield. A Gorgoneion device of this kind, surrounded by three revolving wings, is all that remains of a shield from the first half of the 6th century B.C. (fig. 56). Another shield device, however, far more elaborate and fearful, unique of its kind, has reached us in excellent condition. It consists of a monstrous figure, the like of which is not to be found in the whole of Greek art. The upper part of the composition represents Gorgo holding in her hands two snakes that are coiled around her waist. Her wings grow out of her chest instead of her back. The lower part of her body turns into a sea-dragon at the back, while in front she displays powerful lion's limbs (fig. 67). Could this possibly be a version of *Phobos* (fear) and *Deimos* (terror) which according to Homer, decorated Agamemnon's shield, coupled with Gorgo? Was this strange work fashioned in some workshop of Magna Graecia, as suggested by E. Kunze, the archaeologist who discovered it? Both these suppositions concerning this amazing creation of the mid-6th century B.C. may well be true.

## Architectural bronzes

The imagination of the artists of the Archaic age was inexhaustible, giving a new life to familiar themes, at times in the most unexpected way. The griffin was one of the most popular motifs in early Greek art; Greek artists borrowed it from the East, but transformed it and endowed it with the nobility and dynamism of the Greek form. But the griffin produced by the creator of an early Archaic bronze plate (630-620 B.C.) which perhaps served as a covering for a wooden metope — as its size seems to indicate — is both unique and charming: we are shown a female griffin suckling her young. It is a representation which ennobles the fearful creature by unexpectedly transforming it into an affectionate mother! (fig. 70).

## Tripods

The tripods, the most common votive offerings at Olympia and all the other Greek sanctuaries, are the last to be mentioned here. From early Geometric times onward, the tripod was the votive offering *par excellence*. At first, it was adorned with two large, upright, circular handles (fig. 65), surmounted by small bronze figurines, usually miniature horses with or without a male figure holding them in rein. Later on, the rim of tripods was decorated with busts of griffins, their menacing beaks turned outwards (fig. 71). Finally, the rim came to be adorned with all kinds of other figures, human or animal, such as lions, sphinxes, etc. It is under this highly ornamental and splendid aspect that we must visualize the innumerable bronze tripods of that time, only few of which have reached us intact. However, what has survived are the bronze sheets that decorated the legs of the tripods and the numerous griffin's heads; these enable us to trace with great certainty the constant change and growth of Greek form as it proceeded, with crystalline limpidity, to express the spiritual message of each successive era.

*15. The very ancient temple of Hera (late 7th century B.C.) is situated at the foot of the Kronion hill in the holiest spot of the sacred grove. The Heraion is seen here from the north-east side, with some of its columns restored. In the background, the palaistra is just visible.*

*16*

16. *General view of the valley of Olympia, with the river Alpheios in the background. This is the birthplace of the Olympic spirit which was transmitted from here to the whole world. After the revival of the Olympic Games, the sacred flame is rekindled in the sacred grove every four years and brings the Olympic light to the remotest corners of the world.*

17. *Aerial view of the ancient Altis. The photograph shows the ruins of the temple of Zeus and the Leonidaion (left), the Heraion and the Treasuries (right).*

18. *The temple of Zeus, the largest ancient temple in Peloponnesos was built by the architect Libon of Elis. The surviving pedimental sculptures and metopes are masterpieces of the severe style. The main object of worship in the temple was the gold and ivory statue of Zeus by Pheidias. Only the foundations of the temple have been preserved, together with a large number of architectural parts toppled on the ground.*

19. *The "Metroon," a temple dedicated to the Mother of the Gods, was built east of the Heraion, in the 4th century B.C. It was a small elegant temple in the Doric style. The only remains of this fine building are parts of the stylobate and entablature.*

17

18

19

20. *A section of the Gymnasion of Olympia, built in the 2nd century B.C. The athletes taking part in the Olympic Games used the spacious inner courtyard as a training-ground for running and throwing the javelin or the discus. The Palaistra (the wrestling-ground) was adjacent to the Gymnasion; one can discern it in the background of the picture.*

21. *The Palaistra, built during the Hellenistic period near the river Kladeos, on the western side of the Altis, served both as wrestling-ground and living quarters for the athletes. The square peristyle courtyard was most frequented by the pancratiasts (those who practised the pancration, a combination of wrestling and boxing) and the wrestlers proper. A large part of the Palaistra has been restored.*

22. The "Krỳpte" was the official entrance to the stadion, used by both the Hellanodikai (the chief judges at the Games) and the athletes. The domed passage was built in the Hellenistic period and was subsequently buried under the embankment formed by the west slope of the stadion.

23. The Zanes, i.e. bronze statues of Zeus, were set up in the 4th century B.C. along the road leading from the Altis to the stadion. These statues were made with the fines imposed on athletes who had attempted to gain the title of Olympic victors by dishonest means. The picture shows the stone bases of the statues and the "Krỳpte" in the background.

24. The stadion of Olympia in its present form. It was built in the mid-4th century B.C., outside the sanctuary. The length of the course is about 210 yards, or 600 Olympic feet. The spectators sat on the sloping embankments; on the south side there was a stone platform with seats for the Hellanodikai.

25. *The foundations of the Leonidaion. This large guest-house was built in the mid-4th century B.C., with money offered by the Naxian Leonides, for the purpose of housing official visitors to the Olympic Games.*

26. *This three-aisled Early Christian basilica was built upon the foundations of Pheidias' workshop. The latter had exactly the same dimensions as the sekos of the temple of Zeus, so as to permit Pheidias to work on the great gold and ivory statue of the god within his own workshop.*

26

27. Reproduction of the sacred grove (Altis) as it appeared in Roman times. In the centre, the great temple of Zeus. On the left, the Philippeion and the Heraion; further away, the Nymphaion of Herodes Atticus and the Treasuries. On the east side, the sacred grove was flanked by the stoa of Echo. In the background, a section of the stadion.

28. *General view of the valley of Olympia, with the Alpheios in the background.*

29. *Colossal head of Hera from the cult statue of the goddess that was set up in the Archaic Heraion. Hera was represented seated on her throne and wearing a polos, the sacred headdress worn by numerous female deities. c. 600 B.C.*

30. *Marble head of Alexander the Great.*

31. *Detail from the west pediment of the temple of Zeus. Deidameia.*

29

30

*32. Clay head of Athena. A number of fragments found along with this head suggest that it was part of a votive offering consisting of several figures. The goddess is wearing a diadem decorated with flowers over her finely modelled locks. An outstanding work of the late Archaic period. 490 B.C.*

*33. Figure of Apollo from the west pediment of the temple of Zeus.*

34. *Zeus and Ganymedes. The god, carrying off the beautiful boy, proceeds briskly towards Mount Olympos, to grant him immortality and keep him forever at his side as his personal oinochoos (cupbearer). This clay group of the severe style (470 B.C.) is probably the work of a Corinthian artist, as evidenced by the fine-grained, pale-coloured clay.*

35. *Clay head of a woman. c. 520 B.C.*

35

*36a. The figure of Oinomaos with a himation thrown over his shoulders, leaving his body naked; in his left hand he held his spear, and there was a helmet on his head.*

*36b. Most archaeologists believe that this female figure is Oinomaos' wife Sterope, although a few insist that she is Hippodameia, and should be placed next to Pelops. Sterope (or Hippodameia) is wearing the Doric peplos girded at the waist, and raises her left shoulder in a slightly perplexed manner.*

*37. This figure of the old diviner with his intensely realistic features, dramatic facial expression and eloquent gesture, is one of the finest works among the pedimental sculptures of Olympia and of Greek art in general.*

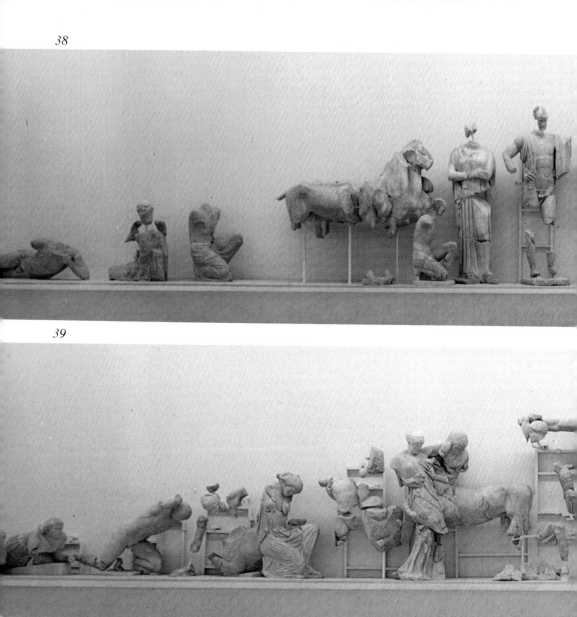

38-39. *The pedimental sculptures of the temple of Zeus are the most impressive group of sculptures in the severe style. The east pediment (fig. 38) illustrates the myth of the chariot race between Oinomaos and Pelops. The artist has depicted the heroes a few moments before the start of the race. In the centre stood the majestic figure of Zeus; to his left and right were the two opposed couples: Oinomaos with his wife Sterope, and Pelops with Oinomaos daughter, Hippodameia. (Archaeologists are in disagreement as to which couple was on the left of Zeus and which on the right). Next to these central figures are depicted the chariots and several auxiliary figures; at the two corners of the pediment, we see the personifications of the two rivers of Olympia, the Alpheios and the Kladeos. The west pediment (fig. 39) represents a Centauromachy. Apollo stands in the centre; to his left and right there are groups of Centaurs and Lapiths, engaged in a fierce fight over the abducted women. The two heroes, Theseus and Peirithoos, stand next to the god. The figures at the two ends of the pediment, of a later date, replaced the original ones, which had been destroyed by some unknown cause. c. 460 B.C.*

40. *Deidameia and the Centaur Eurythion, from the west pediment. This composition was completed by the figure of Peirithoos, his armed right hand raised as he prepares to strike the Centaur who has abducted his young bride during the wedding feast. The young woman struggles to save herself from the inebriated Eurytion; in her effort to free herself, she throws her body forcefully backwards, causing her dress to slip off her shoulder and bare her left breast.*

41. *The figure of Apollo on the west pediment of the temple of Zeus. The god has thrown back his himation over his right shoulder, leaving uncovered his divine body with its sturdy, austere structure and firm flesh. His head is turned to the left, offering the spectator a profile of exceptional sensitivity, in which the compact flesh of the face stands out even more strikingly in contrast with the fluid, well-combed hair. Apollo's right arm is extended towards the group consisting of Peirithoos, Deidameia and Eurytion in a gesture of blessing, indicating the restoration of Apollonian order and the condemnation of the lawless violence of the Centaurs.*

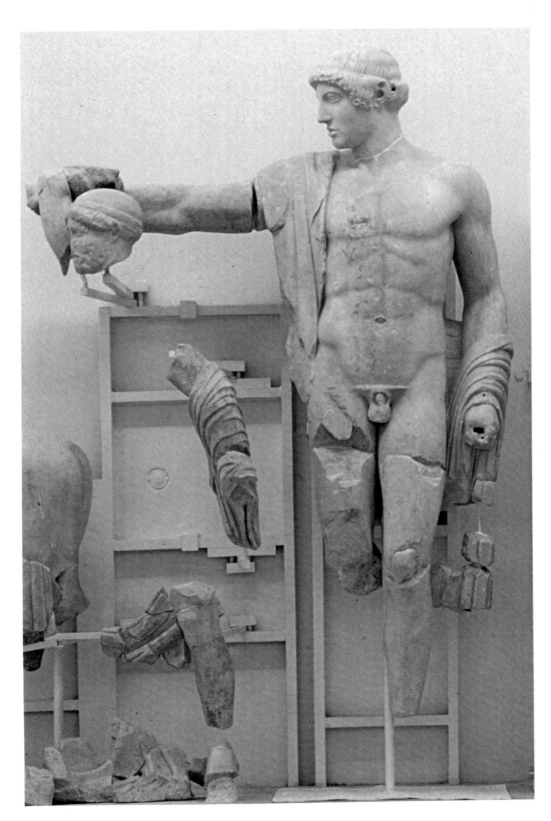

42. *One of the most powerful compositions of the west pediment of the temple of Zeus; a young Lapith is holding a Centaur by the neck in the crook of his right arm; the Centaur has got hold of the youth's arm with both hands and bited into his flesh forcefully. There is an expression of pain on the youth's face rendered by the parted lips, the contraction of the eyes and the wrinkling of the forehead. But the Centaur's rage and pain, as he is caught in the Lapith's strangulating grip, are registered on his brutish face in an equally masterly manner. However, these intensely realistic elements do not deform the two figures or deprive them of their particular characteristics: the nobility and beauty of the young Lapith, the violent bestiality of the mature Centaur.*

43. *A Lapith woman attempts to break away from the violent grip of a Centaur. In her effort, her peplos comes loose over her left shoulder, leaving her youthful breast uncovered. The young woman's posture is quite remarkable, in the way her whole body and the peplos undulate with a rhythm that is both impetuous and disciplined, giving an impression of fluidity, like a sea-wave.*

43

44. *Metope from the east side of the temple of Zeus. It depicts one of the twelve labours of Herakles, the Golden Apples of the Hesperides. The hero has placed a pad on his shoulders; his arms are raised and slightly bent as he carries the tremendous burden of the sky, in the place of Atlas who has gone to fetch the apples for him. Athena stands behind him, lending her support; Atlas has just returned and holds out the palms of his hands, laden with the mythical fruit.*

45. *Metope from the east side of the temple of Zeus. It represents one of Herakles' labours, the cleansing of the Augean stables. Herakles strikes at the bottom of the stable walls with a large lever to make an opening that will let in the waters of the river. Athena stretches out her right hand, pointing at the spot where he must strike.*

46. *Metope from the west side of the temple of Zeus. It records another labour of Herakles, the extermination of the Stymphalian Birds. The hero has slain the dreadful creatures and has come to show his spoils to his patroness, Athena. The goddess, wearing a peplos but not her helmet, the aigis visible on her breast, is seated barefoot upon a rock. This scene has no parallel in the whole of Greek art. (Athena and Herakles' head and right hand are in the Louvre; in the Museum of Olympia these missing pieces have been replaced on the metope by plaster casts.)*

46

47. The Nike (Victory) of Paionios. The statue with its tall triangular pedestal had a total height of 11.90 metres. Her wings extended, her himation spread out and held with her left hand as it billowed out by the wind in her rapid down-ward flight from the sky to the earth, she was shown standing on an eagle. An inscription on the pedestal records that this was a votive offering of the Messenians and the Naupaktians and the work of Paionios of Mende in the Chalkidike peninsula. c. 420 B.C.

48. The Hermes of Pra-xiteles. This famous statue, found in the temple of Hera, shows Hermes holding in his left arm the infant Dio-nysos, while in his raised right hand he probably held a bunch of grapes, dangling it before the childgod, who strecthes out his small hand to grasp the sacred fruit. Hermes has draped his himation over a nearby tree-trunk, revealing his beautiful, houthful body in all its nudity. c. 340 B.C.

49. *An one-winged figure of hammered bronze. A rare example of the hammered bronze technique used by the Greeks in the Archaic period for the production of large bronze statues, prior to the invention of the "cire-perdue" (meltex wax) technique which enabled them to cast statues that were hollow. c. 590-580 B.C.*

50. *Bronze statuette of a warrior carrying a sword. The base supporting the figure leads to the conclusion that together with another figure — that of an old man, also discovered at Olympia — it decorated the rim of a large bronze vessel. It was made in the Lakonian workshop in the mid-6th century B.C.*

51. *Bronze statuette of a young runner at the aphesis, i.e. at the point of starting a race. The inscription on his right thigh reads: TO ΔΙFΟΣΙΜΙ (I belong to Zeus). It was made in the Argive workshop in the early years of the severe style. 480 B.C.*

52. *This bronze horse was part of a votive offering representing a four-horse chariot, probably dedicated by a charioteer who had won a race. It is possibly also a product of the Argive workshop. c. 470-460 B.C.*

*49*

50

51

52

53. Bronze sheet with an embossed representation of two Centaurs hitting a hoplite with fir-trunks. The victim is the mythical hero Kaineas, who was immortal and could be exterminated only if nailed to the ground. c. 630 B.C.

54. Bronze sheet with embossed representation of a warrior about to mount his chariot. His charioteer has already mounted and stands waiting for him; but before leaving for the battle, the warrior turns his head to look at his wife, who is carrying their child on her shoulders. c. 590 B.C.

55. Bronze sheet with embossed representations in two registers. The lower one shows Theseus abducting Antiope; the upper one Orestes killing his mother Klytaimnestra. c. 570 B.C.

56

57

56. Shield device. A gorgoneion encircled by three revolving wings. First half of the 6th century B.C.

57. Bronze greaves; one of these was dedicated to Zeus by the Kleonaians. Second half of the 6th century B.C.

58. Bronze breastplate from a hoplite's armour (early 6th century B.C.). Its simple ornamentation, subordinated to the main formal elements and functional requirements of the object, raise it to the level of a work of art.

59. A fine bronze breastplate with engraved representations. The lower part shows Apollo with his lyre and two Hyperborean maidens, then Zeus with two youths; the upper part depicts lions, bulls, sphinxes and leopards. A little later than the mid-7th century B.C.

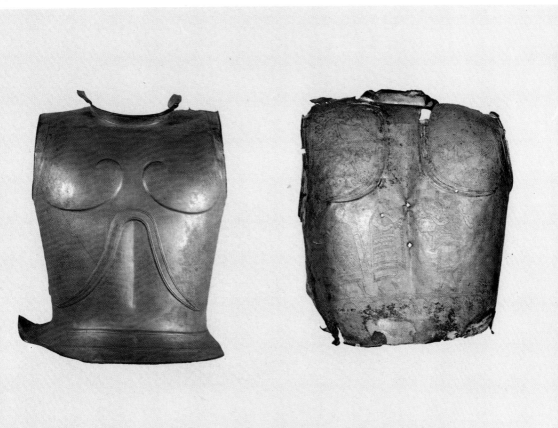

60. *Miltiades' helmet. After the battle of Marathon, the victorious general dedicated it to Zeus, as recorded by the inscription:* ΜΙΛΤΙΑΔΕΣ ΑΝΕΘΕΚΕΝ ΤΟΙ ΔΙΙ. *490 B.C.*

61. *Persian helmet; there is an inscription round the lower edge:* ΔΙΙ ΑΘΕΝΑΙΟΙ ΜΕΔΟΝ ΛΑΒΟΝΤΕΣ (*To Zeus from the Athenians, who took it from the Medes*), *which indicated that it was part of the spoils from the battle of Marathon. 490 B.C.*

62. *Bronze Corinthian helmet. Second half of the 7th century B.C.*

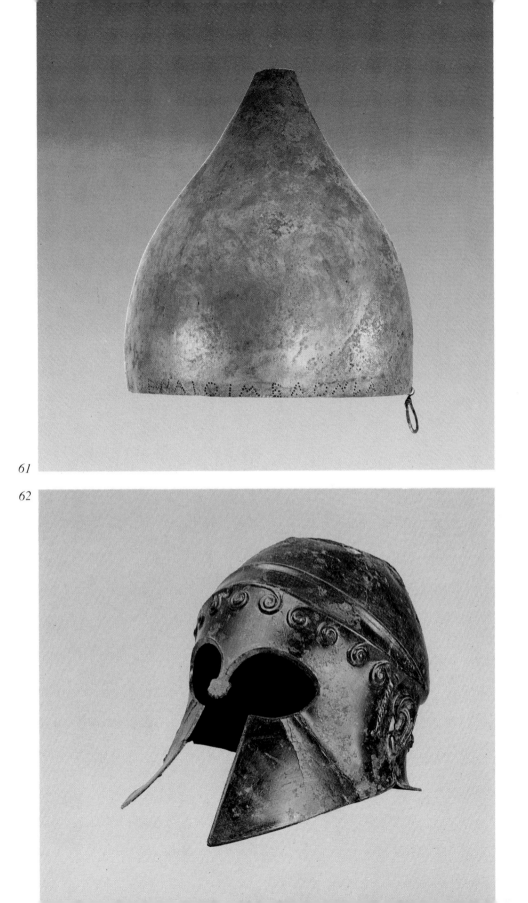

61

62

63. *Bronze helmet of the Illyrian type. The frontal section is decorated with applied silver animals (two lions on either side of a boar). The cheek-piece is decorated with the applied silver figure of a horseman. 530 B.C.*

64. *Bronze helmet of the "Illyrian" type, with rams heads on the cheek-pieces. 6th century B.C.*

65. *Two heraldic sphinxes. They were attached to the rim of a large bronze vessel. 600-550 B.C.*

66. *Bronze tripod of the 9th century B.C. Innumerable tripods of this kind were dedicated to the Altis, the sacred grove at Olympia.*

65

66

67. *A shield device unique in its theme and in the quality of its workmanship: Gorgo with wings growing out of her breast, girded with serpents, the lower part of her body ending in a dragon's tail and lion's legs. Mid-6th century B.C.*

68. *Bronze statuette of an old man. From a Lakonian workshop. C. 550 B.C.*

69. *Bronze statuette of a male figure. 8th century B.C.*

68

69

*70. Bronze sheet; it probably covered a wooden metope. Its subject is unusual and unexpected: a female griffin nursing her young. The fruitful imagination, the profoundly human sensitiveness of the Greek artist thus transformed the ferocious imaginary bird, borrowed from Oriental art, into a peaceful and loving creature. c. 630-620 B.C.*

71. *Head of a griffin; together with other similar figures, it was attached to the rim of a votive tripod. 7th century B.C.*

72. *Bronze sphinx, once attached to some object as a decoration. It is wearing a* polos *on its head, and a ribbon round the forehead to tie up its hair which falls in curls on the forehead, the breast and down the back. From a Lakonian workshop. C. 540-530 B.C.*

73. *Bronze composition of lions tearing apart a dog.*

72

73